Animals of Africa

LEVEL  READER

READING LEVEL
2
GRADES 1 TO 3

Written by Kathryn Knight
Illustrated by Edizioni Larus S.p.A.

bendon®

The Savanna

Leopard

Giraffe

Springbok
Gazelle

Zebra

Cheetah

The wild animals of Africa are amazing!
Many live on the grassy savanna, where it is hot most of the time. There are not many trees on the savanna. Animals must blend in with the grass and bushes to hide— or they must run very fast!

Rhinoceros

Warthog

Sable Antelope

Lion

Elephant

The African elephant is the largest land animal in the world. Elephants live in groups called herds. The babies are called calves. Look at those long trunks! Elephants use their trunks to suck up water, squirt themselves to cool off, and reach the leaves on tall tree branches.

Rhinoceros

The African rhinoceros is a huge, fast animal. The rhino doesn't see well, but it does have a big, sharp horn to protect itself. It eats grass, twigs, leaves, and fruit. When it gets hot on the African savanna, the rhino takes a cool mud bath.

Giraffe

The giraffe is a tall, graceful animal. It eats leaves, which it can reach with its l-o-n-g neck and long tongue. The giraffe spends its whole life on its feet. When it sleeps, it bends its neck, touching the ground with its head.

Zebra

Zebras belong to the same animal group as horses and donkeys. Look at those black and white stripes. Those stripes confuse the animals that hunt zebras. When the zebras are in a herd, they all blend together, and it's hard to pick out just one.

A baby zebra is called a foal.

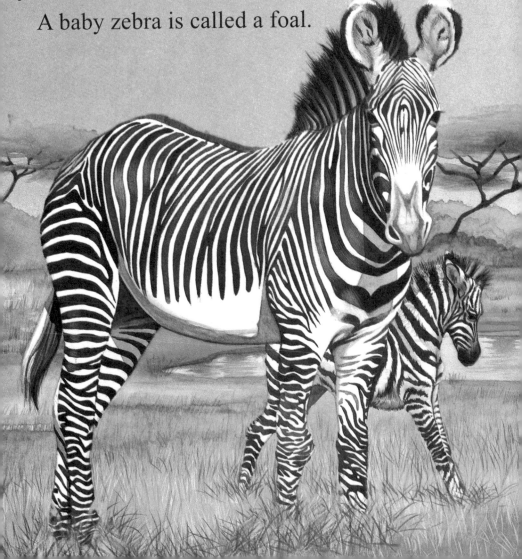

Lion

The lion is the largest, strongest cat in Africa. It is called the king of the beasts. Lions live in groups called prides. Babies are called cubs. When it's very hot, lions nap on tree branches or rest near water. Male lions sleep about 20 hours a day and hunt at night.

African Hunting Dog

The biggest dogs in the world are the African hunting dogs. They have long legs, rounded ears, and spotted coats.

They hunt in packs, and they talk to each other by squeaking or chirping like birds.

Gnu

This odd-looking animal is a gnu (pronounced "new") or wildebeest (**will**-da-beast). Gnus live in huge herds—up to 200,000! They are often hunted by lions and other animals. They stay together, moving from one grassy area to the next. Gnus can go without water for five days.

Ostrich

The ostrich is the largest bird in the world. It can run as fast as a horse! But, even though it has wings, it can't fly.

Ostriches have just two toes on each foot. The biggest one has a long claw that is used to kick at enemies.

The Forest

Pelican

Hippopotamus

Crowned
Crane

Crocodile

Many animals live in the warm, rainy
African forests. There is plenty of water
and things to eat here—leaves,
fruits, and insects.

Scaly
Anteater

Gorilla

Chimpanzee

Flamingo

Chimpanzee

Chimpanzees are apes, not monkeys.
They do not have tails. They are very clever—
clever enough to make simple tools! A chimp
can use a long stick to get at juicy termites.

Baby chimpanzees like to ride "piggyback"
as their mothers hunt for insects, leaves,
and bananas to eat.

Gorilla

Gorillas are the biggest apes in the world. They can weigh more than 400 pounds! They live in small groups, eating mostly leaves and fruits.

The males, called silverbacks, protect their families by pretending to attack. They stand up, rip up bushes, and yell and pound on their chests!

Hippopotamus

The hippopotamus is one of Africa's biggest animals. It lives near rivers and lakes. It has webbed feet to help it swim and can hold its breath under water for up to 25 minutes! *Hippopotamus* comes from Greek words meaning "river horse."

Bongo

The bongo is a kind of antelope. In fact, it is the largest antelope in the African forest.

Baby bongos are called fawns. Bongos can leap well and run very fast to escape other animals. Bongos like to munch on bamboo, grass, and beans.

Python

What's up in that tree? It's very still...but it is hungry. It's watching and waiting for an animal meal to walk by. It can wait a long time. It can go a year without eating! It's a python—one of the largest snakes in the world. Be careful!

Crocodile

Many rivers and lakes of Africa are home to this large reptile—the crocodile!

Crocodiles stay on the riverbank in the warm sun, or float near the top of the water, waiting for an unlucky animal to walk by. They strike quickly with their strong jaws and sharp teeth!

Madagascar

Fossa

Indri

Madagascar
is a large island
off the coast of Africa.
There are animals here
that live nowhere else
on Earth.

Chameleon

Tenrec
Hedgehog

Sifaka
Lemur

There are
many lemurs, which are
similar to monkeys. They have
strong legs and can leap from
one tree to another.

Ring-tailed
Lemur

The Desert

Addax
Antelope

Arabian
Camel

Fennec
Fox

Sand Skink

Many parts of Africa stay dry most of the year. Yet there are animals that find a way to live in these deserts. They eat insects and grass, when they can find it. And they need very little water.

Berber Goat

Gemsbok

Yellow Scorpion

Meerkat

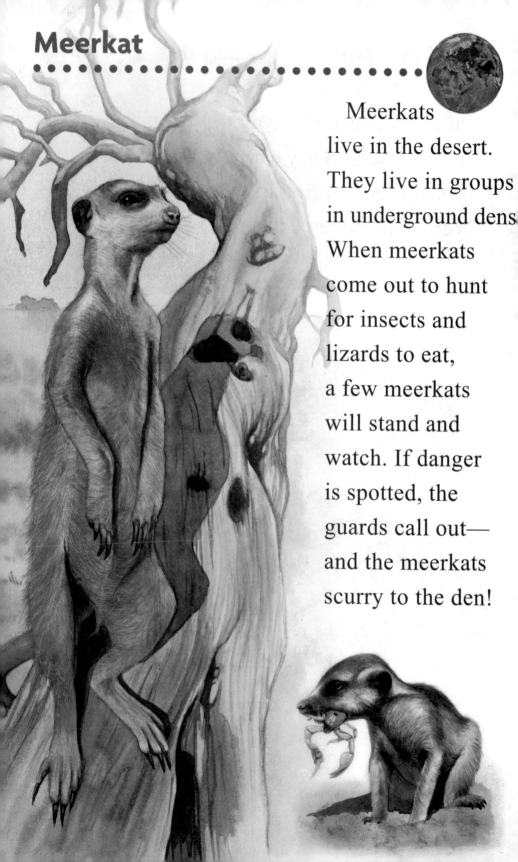

Meerkats live in the desert. They live in groups in underground dens. When meerkats come out to hunt for insects and lizards to eat, a few meerkats will stand and watch. If danger is spotted, the guards call out— and the meerkats scurry to the den!